Is
This
You?

Katy Knapman

Grosvenor House
Publishing Limited

This book is published by
Grosvenor House Publishing Ltd
Link House
140 The Broadway, Tolworth, Surrey, KT6 7HT.
www.grosvenorhousepublishing.co.uk

A CIP record for this book
is available from the British Library

ISBN 978-1-80381-174-1

For George Alifragkis,
a loyal friend,
a wise speaker,
a pure soul.

In the entirety of our universe,
I am ever grateful that I got to meet you.

Contents

Introduction

As Bob Proctor declares, '*this is an orderly universe*'.
Nothing happens by accident, you have not
stumbled across this book accidentally. You are here for a
reason. That reason is to learn how to use the power within
you to achieve the life you wish for.
Own what you wish to have.
Become the person you aspire to be.

For years strong scientific research has been conducted to provide us with evidence that explains how the universe works. Research suggests that the many particles that we are made up of and that are contained inside of us, have existed for millions of millennia. In fact, the hydrogen inside of us was produced by the Big Bang, while the carbon, nitrogen and oxygen that flows through us were produced in burning stars. The heaviest particles inside of us were simply made of exploding stars. In other words, we are made up of stardust from the universe.

We are stars of the universe, constantly shining. The stars you wish upon, that you believe create miracles and dreams to come true, are made up of the same stuff that you are made up of. You have the exact power inside of you gifted from the universe, you are born with magic. The star you wish upon in the night sky holds the same power as you do to bring your dreams into reality. You are a magical star. You have magic inside of you.

This is not a philosophy, this is physics.

Stars are the main components of galaxies and were among the first objects to form in the early universe. The closest star to Earth is the Sun. Think how powerful and strong the Sun is. It is 150.73 million km away from Earth, yet still radiates us with warmth. The Sun is so powerful and yet it is simply a star, just like us. We have the same potential to radiate our own energy. As we are part of the universe, just like the other components, we have the natural ability to convert our energies. Simply, we are energy conversion machines. We can convert our energy any way we wish, and this determines the outcome of our life.

Theorists believe that stars form dark matter. Dark matter consists of particles that do not absorb, reflect or emit light. These particles were created at the very beginning of the universe and exist free-floating throughout space. Dark matter has influenced the evolution of the universe. It has shaped entire galaxies without touching anything. Astrophysicists admit that most galaxies would probably not have formed exactly how they have without dark matter. It is obvious how powerful and mysterious dark matter is. It holds the power and answers to so many unexplained and magical occurrences. To be specific, 80% of the universe is made up of dark matter. The entire universe is full of dark matter or in other words, full of magic. The weight of dark matter is so light, it is able to escape into space and can float anywhere. This means magic exists within us and all around us, naturally.

We have been created with so many magical particles that still exist inside of us, we hold so much potential, so much energy and so much power. We are made from stardust, formed in the same way dark matter is. As we live, we are constantly being showered in particles of dark matter. What makes you think you do not have the power to live the way you dream to live or to achieve all that you desire? You are already halfway towards living the life you dream of as you naturally hold the magic and power within you. You are part of the universe.

> This book has been created to help you self-reflect and designed to help you use your magic that you consist of, that you are born with, to live the life you desire. But only if you want it.

Everything is Energy

As Hans Andewig says, '*everything comes
from the same source and returns to it*'.
You are the source. Therefore, whatever energy you
put out, you will attract back. If you feel good,
you attract good. If you feel bad, you attract bad.
We are magnetic to what we distribute.

As you are now aware, we are formed of atoms. Essentially,
we are big balls of energy. We also know how real energy is.
We can feel when someone is staring at us. We can feel
energy in a room. Energy influences us, our situations and
our emotions. As we are one with the universe, we are one
with the universal energy field.

Energy is connected to vibration. Vibration is the vibrating
movement of particles caused by energy. Energy creates the
particles to move (vibrate) in accordance to a vibrational
frequency. Frequency is what determines the rate at which
the vibrations occur. Frequencies can distinguish vibrational
patterns, for instance, energy that is vibrating faster would
be a higher frequency than one that is vibrating at a slower

1

pace. Taking the two together, we can have either a high vibration or a low vibration. Our energy produces vibrations and the frequency of these vibrations can determine the events and outcome of our life. The only thing you can grow is what you feed with energy. Our energy manifests our life's sequels. Our life is the after-effect of our energy.

We must be mindful of our energy.

Energy is always influenced by your mind and therefore determines the outcome of your life. Your mind is your only limitation in life, whatever you think, you feel, you live. You are your only limit. Your thoughts, beliefs and habits could either be limiting you from a high vibration or resonating with a high vibration. If you feel good, you think good, you live good. It works the opposite way; if you feel bad, you think bad, you live bad.

ACTIVITY

Check in with yourself.

Use a notebook and dedicate it to the activities within this book. On the first page I want you to write, 'It's on me, *[insert your name],* to get me where I want to be'.

Sit down and take three deep breaths, in through the nose, out through the nose.

Notice how you feel. Write down how you feel at this moment. Give this feeling a rating out of 10, with 0 being low and 10 being fantastic, and write down the rating.

Now write down the reasons for why you feel this way. Ask yourself:

– What thoughts are on my mind?
– What beliefs do you have about yourself?
– What evidence is there for the way you feel and think?
– What habits are limiting yourself from being a high 10?

Whatever you are feeling is created by energy. Your thoughts, beliefs and habits may be limiting your vibration. If you are vibrating low it is easy and natural to project it onto external reasons, creating excuses and fulfilling the limiting circle. The limiting circle is a continuous circle that you have built yourself. What goes round in this circle is an external reason for your own thoughts, feelings, beliefs and habits.

The diagrams below compare energy circles.

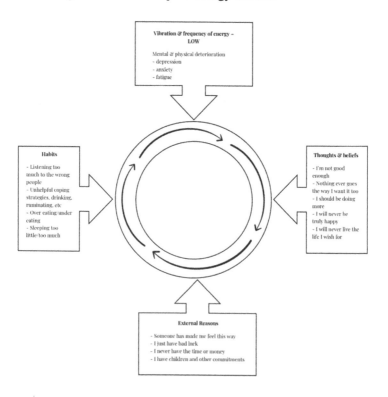

Vibration & frequency of energy – LOW

Mental & physical deterioration
- depression
- anxiety
- fatigue

Habits

- Listening too much to the wrong people
- Unhelpful coping strategies, drinking, ruminating, etc
- Over eating/under eating
- Sleeping too little/too much

Thoughts & beliefs

- I'm not good enough
- Nothing ever goes the way I want it too
- I should be doing more
- I will never be truly happy
- I will never live the life I wish for

External Reasons

- Someone has made me feel this way
- I just have bad luck
- I never have the time or money
- I have children and other commitments

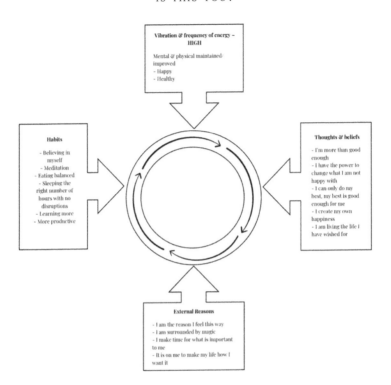

Vibration & frequency of energy – HIGH

Mental & physical maintained/improved
- Happy
- Healthy

Habits

- Believing in myself
- Meditation
- Eating balanced
- Sleeping the right number of hours with no disruptions
- Learning more
- More productive

Thoughts & beliefs

- I'm more than good enough
- I have the power to change what I am not happy with
- I can only do my best, my best is good enough for me
- I create my own happiness
- I am living the life I have wished for

External Reasons

- I am the reason I feel this way
- I am surrounded by magic
- I make time for what is important to me
- It is on me to make my life how I want it

The Power of Self-Awareness

Self-awareness is the ability to focus on yourself and how your actions, thoughts, or emotions do or do not align with your lifestyle.

If you really are wanting to become your best self, to improve your lifestyle, your relationships, social life or maybe just to improve your confidence and master self-love, a journey to within is vital. So often people go on journeys to places, they may learn and discover something new there – but so often people do not go on journeys within to learn and discover something new about themselves. We must be self-aware to learn, grow and achieve.

Are you responsible for what you are feeling now, for the thoughts and beliefs you have of yourself and how you are living your life? Your life is a sum of your choices and decisions. Whether or not you have made good choices and decisions, whether you like the person you are now or are lacking confidence in aspects of your life, it does not matter as you have the power to change anything you wish. You have the power to become who you aspire to be and live how you want to live. It is not anyone else's fault as to why you are living your life how you are, no one is responsible for someone else.

It's is on you to take responsibility and to change your life.

How can you expect to grow and achieve the life you want or become the person you aspire to be if you are not looking at yourself first? Moreover, how can you improve aspects of your life if you have not stopped to consider your own individual actions and behaviours? These thoughts, beliefs, habits and actions dominate your life. It is so easy to feel frustrated with other people or situations you are faced with but have you taken the time to figure out why? Even though this can be hard to accept, the answer is that it all starts with you. Do not be frustrated with other people but be frustrated with yourself because this is when self-development really happens. You cannot control other people or any external forces but you are in control of yourself and while external things do happen, you are in charge with how you perceive and respond to them. Your best freedom in life is how you choose to respond to things. No matter the circumstances you face, you have the creative capacity to create change, based on your own perceptions which motivate your response. Your response is charged by your energy. It is on you, as to how you perceive and respond to external forces.

Self-awareness allows us to grow. Just by growing, our lives improve and become meaningful. If life was consistently smooth sailing, we would never reach our higher self, our most powerful version of who we are. Life would be mundane, the person you would become would be boring. We gain a sense of meaning through the lessons we learn and the person we become. Robin Sharma once said, '*If you are not scared, you are not growing*'. If the decisions you are making and the dreams you are visioning are not scaring you then you will be limiting yourself from reaching your potential and the life you wish for. The struggles in life that you have experienced make you who you are and make you powerful. We have become far stronger because of our faults and our trauma than we have from the good moments in life. Living through the bad teaches you how strong you are, shows you what you are capable of and that you have the courage inside of you to feel, face and manage fear. You have nothing to fear because you are all you need to get through anything that comes your way. To grow, you must get real with yourself. It is critical to be self-aware as this allows you to understand yourself and to create changes that support the life you wish for.

We could say 'I am who I am and I am enough' but we should instead say 'I am who I am, I am enough and I want to always be the best I can be'. Live outside of your comfort zone and grow. Grow to get the life you desire. Self-awareness is the ultimate key to living your best life. By wanting the best for ourselves means to work on ourselves. Once we have understood one part of ourselves, there is always something else that we can acknowledge that we do not fully understand. This is a constant cycle. We are forever changing because our external world is forever changing. Therefore, we cannot expect to understand ourselves or love ourselves to the ultimate level because we are not in control of life. We must move with life; we must be willing to change and take responsibility. You will grow, learn to love yourself and live the life you wish for if you are self-aware.

ACTIVITY

In your notebook note three scenarios where you took criticism well.

Note three scenarios where you were proud of yourself, not for what you have achieved but for how you behaved.

Note three scenarios where you did not respond well and underneath write how you wish to respond if this scenario happens again.

Write a paragraph describing yourself, including things like, your average mood, your habits, your values.

Are you accepting and appreciating criticism?
Are you behaving considerately?
The person you are right now, is this you?

Alter Ego

It was Ayesha Siddiqi who said,
'be who you needed when you were younger'.

Anita Quansah said, *'to be your best
self you must visualise your higher
self and start showing up as her'.*

Sometimes we are faced with scenarios that feel uneasy. Perhaps you had an argument with someone important and it got out of control, you responded in a way that you regret. Perhaps you made a mistake and didn't quite find the right amendment. Perhaps you aren't fulfilling your potential, or an external force is delaying you from being where you want to be. Maybe you are delaying yourself from getting to where you want to be.

When we are in these uneasy times, we must remember that it is okay to make mistakes, we are human not robots. Striving for perfectionism is simply a desperation to feel safe and this is only a short term feeling of safety. We need to become safe with our imperfections and accepting of our mistakes. There is part of our brain that produces the feelings of fear and doubt. There is a voice that encourages shame, doubt, guilt, worry and desperation. We can easily become the victim to our own voices, we can so easily be filled with guilt and shame. Sometimes we can be so suffocated that we have prolific doubt or we react and respond to scenarios in ways that do not seem true to ourselves.

Our consciousness can connect to our higher self. We can become really creative with becoming consciously aware of our behaviour. We can express ourselves, use our imagination and intuition. Susan Jeffers said, *'by learning to trust your intuition, miracles seem to happen'*. Intuitive thoughts are gifts from the higher self. To reduce the number of uneasy situations or doubtful voices, you must use your higher self.

As stated previously, we are literal balls of energy. Living by our higher self raises our vibration. When living by your higher self, your vibration will be so high that you will find yourself receiving more miracles every day. Your higher self is the part of you that can manipulate your source and therefore your vibration. View your higher self as an alter ego; an alternative you. I like to consider my alter ego as a close friend, someone who always inspires me, someone I am in absolute awe of. This way I can really distinguish my true self from my false self and most importantly I can respond to scenarios in the best and truest possible way.

ACTIVITY

Take a moment to think about who you have always looked up to. Who is someone that has always inspired you?

Either draw a picture of them or stick a photo of them in the middle of the page in your notebook. At the top of the page give this person, your alter ego, a name. Create a name or keep the name the same as the person who inspires you.

Write down words that describe this person around the photo.

Write down as many reasons as to why they inspire you.

Write down three ways how you are not resonating with this person.

Now that you are self-aware, your goal is to think of how this person may respond in certain scenarios that you have experienced or may experience.

Write down three ways this person would respond to your scenarios.

When you face uneasy situations or you are hearing voices, think of your alter ego.
What would they do?

Is this you showing up for yourself?
Is this you living your higher self?

Your Assertive Rights

People too often forget that it is your
own choice to live how you want to spend
the rest of your life.

We have all been faced with dilemmas which we find hard to produce a correct response or outcome, or where rights and wrongs become perplexing. Although as individuals we all have specific beliefs, values and morals, so rights and wrongs are in fact an illusion. There is no such thing as absolutely right, nor is there such a thing as absolutely wrong. Even though it can be hard to grasp this statement, because of these individual beliefs, values and morals, rights and wrongs consequently become entirely subjective. One act of desirable behaviour can be the anticipation of adhering to society's values but when it comes to precise situations it can be difficult to feel confident with your chosen action or reaction. This is where your assertive rights can be helpful. Being aware of your rights will instantly reinforce your inner assurance and empower your individual morale.

Live according to the following statements of your rights:

- I have a right to be treated with respect.
- I have a right to say no without feeling guilty.
- I have a right to experience and express my feelings.
- I have a right to take time and think.
- I have a right to change my mind.
- I have a right to ask for what I want.
- I have a right to ask for information.
- I have a right to do less than I am humanly capable of doing.
- I have a right to make mistakes.
- I have a right to feel good about myself.
- I have a right to do what makes me happy.
- I have a right to make my own decisions.
- I have a right to do things other people do not approve of.

These are solely yours to use. Look in the mirror and say them to yourself, believe in them and most importantly live by them. This technique can even help with identifying your emotions in which some may be hard to accept or perform. Do recognise that assertive rights also apply to other people, whether they are close to you or people you do not know. Everyone is entitled to equality. Therefore, as you have the right to change your mind about something or to express your feelings deservedly, so do other people.

Now look at other people's assertive rights below:

- Other people have the right to be treated with respect.
- Other people have a right to say no without feeling guilty.
- Other people have a right to experience and express their feelings.
- Other people have a right to take time and think.
- Other people have a right to change their minds.
- Other people have a right to ask for what they want.
- Other people have a right to ask for information.
- Other people have a right to do less than they are humanly capable of doing.
- Other people have a right to make mistakes.
- Other people have a right to feel good about themselves.
- Other people have a right to do what makes them happy.
- Other people have a right to make their own decisions.
- Other people have a right to do things of which I may not approve.

Now that both are listed you can start to analyse past, present and future situations to form personal growth and acceptance. Being consciously aware of everyone's assertive rights will result in applied equality. The base of all healthy relationships is formed by mutual respect, this technique will encourage functional aspects to relationships by being able to pay attention to what is right for you and what is right for other people.

Finding the balance between being assertive and using your assertive rights appropriately can be challenging. I have created an assertive rights spectrum which will help you in your righteous journey to assertiveness (see the diagram). To gather an insight as to where you fall on the spectrum, ask yourself; do you stand up for yourself? Or do you have the tendency to only think of your own opinion and forget about other people having their own rights?

The Assertive Rights Spectrum

Passive	Assertive	Aggressive
Overly nice despite true feelings	Firm	Arrogant and cold
Low self-esteem	Self-confident	Overly high self-esteem
Powerless	Powerful	Manipulative
Latent hostility	Comfortable	Hostile
Weak boundaries	Clear and defined boundaries	Overpowering, low consideration of others
Pushover	Content	Controlling
Passive	Active	Attacking
Dependent	Independent	Disorganised behaviour
Approval-seeking	Self-sufficient	Power-seeking

At the bottom end of the spectrum is being passive; this is when an individual is predominantly passive. The life of the individual holds weak to no boundaries; therefore, the individual may feel as if they are powerless and perhaps struggle with low self-esteem. Whereas, at the other end of the assertive spectrum is being aggressive; this is when an individual is predominantly aggressive. The individual could possibly be perceived as selfish, holding no consideration for others. Therefore, boundaries are consistently broken. To the extreme at this end of the spectrum, the personality of this individual would appear to be overbearing, leading to a hostile and controlling lifestyle. The middle point on this spectrum is being assertive, to get to this point an individual must be respectful and self-sufficient. To maintain their position on the spectrum, the individual has to be self-aware at all times. It is on you to set clear boundaries, if someone crosses these boundaries, it is on you to have the self-esteem to decide the best movement for your own self.

I would like to acknowledge that your boundaries are never 'stupid'. You are your own person and you have the right to define these boundaries as you wish. The boundary for one person may be different to that of another person, but all boundaries should be recognised and respected as they are individually meaningful. The ultimate destination of assertiveness is living a comfortable and content lifestyle.

ACTIVITY

Imagine you are 18 years old and your parents are passing you a passport. On this passport it says 'Your life'. You take the passport.

This passport is the pass and freedom to life, you can do whatever you wish and go where you desire. You have the absolute freedom to behave, think, feel and speak however you wish. You have the freedom to make your own choices, own decisions and live exactly how you want too.

Describe your life. Write about how you are living your life, what your daily routine is, what beliefs you hold, what career you have and what types of friends you have.

Compare it to your life now – are you living how you want to live?

If you feel as if you are living your life by someone else's rules, write down what specific assertive right(s) can bring that power back to you.

Are you asserting yourself to achieve your desired lifestyle? The freedom to behave, decide, think, feel and speak has been given to you so is this you and your life?

Priorities

Our habits influence our life.
Our habits naturally form our priorities.
Our habits control our priorities.
Our priorities determine our lifestyle.
Our habits and priorities can waste our potential.

Subconsciously, our habits encourage our mindset. Our daily habits hold the control over the outcome of not only our mindset but also our day-to-day life. If our habits are healthy and bring out the ultimate potential in us, then our life flourishes as a result. On the other hand, if our habits are unhealthy, our mindset is negatively impacted and our potential and lifestyle are limited. Our habits and our priorities determine our mindset and our mindset determines the energy we vibrate and therefore, our life. It is obvious that the single greatest power we all have is our mind, our mind determines 95% of our life while the other 5% is determined by our strategies. The plan of actions we have for ourselves only influences 5% of our life. To put it another way, if your habits are healthy and you are happy, you are emitting a high frequency of energy to manifest. The more you prioritise forming healthy habits, the happier you will be and the higher energy you will vibrate, so abundant miracles will be received.

I once took a trip to a grocery shop and got talking to a man behind the tills. He told me he was working there part-time but before he worked at the shop, he was a successful lawyer who had his own law firm. I asked him why he gave up his law firm and he told me the story. Before he decided to study law at university, he went for an interview with a top London broker firm. The first question they asked him was, 'If money were no object, what would you buy?' The man replied, 'a house'. His interview was cut short after his reply and a few days later he was contacted to be told his interview was unsuccessful and he did not get the job. He called them up and asked how he could have improved and they told him that he was too comfortable, too stable. The worker was left feeling confused, he always thought stability was an appealing quality to have. He dwelled for weeks, wondering what kind of answer they were looking for. A month later at a networking event he bumped into the man who interviewed him. The broker told the worker the answer they were looking for was a fast car or something similarly expensive and dispensable. The worker asked why and the broker said, because it is not stable, it is materialistic and they know that a young ambitious man who desires such materialism is going to keep wanting more. The worker then figured that the firm was trying to figure out how driven an interviewee is for the purpose of money. For example, a man driven by materialistic things is going to want a faster car or designer clothes to wear and this way of living is going to make the company more money. Videlicet, the more ambitious, the more money earnt and the more the firm gains.

Years later the worker had graduated and was sitting in his office of his own law firm where he had run his business successfully for over ten years. Although his business was successful, his marriage was crumbling and his wife was about to leave him. His social life was non-existent and he had been suffering with migraines for months. With the threat of his wife leaving due to never spending quality time together, the worker sat at his desk and asked himself, 'will owning this business and earning this money make my soul happy?' Within weeks he sold his business and went home to his wife. They managed to rekindle their love, they had a party to go to every month and he felt refreshed and stress free, so much so that his migraines magically stopped.

The worker told me, you can work so hard to try and achieve happiness but you sell your soul. When it comes to business it is all about money, companies will take and take and take. He said companies are not afraid to take your happiness, your life and your soul if money is being earnt. You will lose everything to earn money and even when you have money to spend, it is only a short fix; it is not long-term happiness. The happiness lasts a few days maximum and then you go through the same process again to lose more of yourself, only to get another short fix. The worker learnt the biggest lesson of his life, prioritise what makes your soul happy. A simple shift in perspective is all it takes for you to get your priorities right. Do not work hard, work smart. Always put your happiness before money and be confident in believing that the money will always follow.

ACTIVITY

Answer the following questions:

1. What does your dream lifestyle look like?
2. Why do you live your life how you live it now?
3. Is this how you want to live your life?
4. What habits do you perform to help bring out your potential?
5. What limitations are you causing yourself?

Is this you making yourself happy?

Searching for Meaning and Purpose

Happiness is a journey not a destination.
Happiness is to be found along the way and not
at the end of the road, for then the journey is over
and is too late. The time for happiness is now,
today, not tomorrow.

If we dig deep and think about the mistakes we have made, and particularly think about how we felt after the mistakes, we can gain a sense of perspective. Many of the mistakes we have made leave us feeling shameful, regretful, guilty and other such emotions but in the same given moment we also gained meaning through learning a lesson. We often get so caught up in the negative emotions associated with mistake making that we overlook it as a gift, it is healthy to make mistakes. Mistakes are simply a reminder of the path towards which we are heading. Evolutionary psychologists believe that our brains can recall bad memories easier than good memories but also intensify those bad memories more than the good memories. If we shift our perspective and accept that we made a mistake, we can also identify a lesson which changes our mindset and emotions, perhaps even habits. The reason I speak of this is because we gain more meaning and purpose from life through challenges and suffering than we do when life is content. Of course, it does not seem at the time of suffering that we are indeed growing and this can be one of the hardest notions to come to terms with. It should be noted that time does not heal our sufferings, rather, it is what we do with our time that our suffering can in turn develop and we can grow with our choices that we make during this challenging but vital time.

How we respond to these mistakes is vital in the search for meaning and purpose. Do you look for the meaning behind a mistake or a tough situation or do you find yourself dwelling and complaining about it? You have a choice. Between external circumstances and your response lies a gap for your own choice. A choice on how you internalise the circumstance and how you respond to it. Everything can be taken from you but one thing – the freedom to choose your attitude. You and you alone will decide what your life will be like in the next given moment. You can find meaning in life even if you are suffering, facing horrendous circumstances or have experienced serious trauma, it comes down to how you respond. The situation is irrelevant, it is simply about you and your attitude. When we are unable to change a situation, we are challenged to change ourselves. Finding meaning and purpose can only happen when you aim at your greater cause, at the bigger picture. We must allow ourselves time to feel raw emotions then it comes down to our choice and personal freedom to adjust our attitude.

Viktor Frankl published a book about this concept of finding meaning in the suffering of life. He wrote, 'you can either make a victory of your experiences or you can ignore the challenge and simply live mundanely. Suffering should be seen as a task, one that provides you with an opportunity for achievement, you can find meaning and hidden opportunities in any challenge and suffering'. To illustrate this perception of suffering, we must ask ourselves why we choose to live when we are suffering? Nietzsche says, 'he who has a reason to live can bear almost any how'. What is the reason you decide to live? The reason or reasons you think of provides your purpose. You have granted yourself a purpose to live and can experience absurd challenges throughout life but this purpose will remain with you and guide you.

For those of us who struggle to feel any sense of meaning to life, Dr Robert Waldinger had a goal to understand what makes a meaningful life and what keeps people happy. Waldinger conducted the most extensive and prolonged studies of adult development and life. To attain the clearest understanding of adult development, he studied participants from diverse socio-economic backgrounds, from their teenage years into their old age over a period of 83 years. The study resulted in one main finding – good relationships keep us happier and healthier. For those who participated, not only were interviews conducted but science was used to measure happiness throughout their entire lives using blood samples, brain scans and medical record tracking.

Ultimately, science discovered that the thing needed to make a meaningful life is simply connection. To have a long and fulfilling life, science claims you must be securely connected to at least one other person. Sometimes it can be hard to find someone to connect with, to build and maintain a relationship with. This makes it harder for us to connect and consequently attempt to live a meaningful life through science. Yet, if we do the things we love, we are more likely to attract and connect with other people. Moreover, other people can enjoy and connect with your energy. If you were to invest now into something that would make your soul happy, where would you put your time and your energy? Question the things you know about yourself and the world to really understand, what makes your soul happy.

Research has established that social connection not only heightens our self-esteem and regulates our emotions, the power of connection also lowers our anxiety and depression. It is clear the desire to connect is not only a naturally occurring human drive but also a core human need. By neglecting our drive to connect, we neglect the feeling of belonging to something greater than oneself. Just like any other social animal, without connecting we naturally suffer mentally, emotionally and physically. Despite this natural desire to connect, we are living in a time of true disconnect. With the current worldwide population at 7.75 billion, 5.19 billion people are active on social media. An average mobile phone user opens WhatsApp 23–25 times a day. While 2021 statistics vary for different countries, UK citizens are spending an average of 3 hours 40 minutes on social media. When compared to the 2012 UK statistics, citizens were spending an average of an hour on social media. It is evident we are spending even more time behind our phones and computers, consequently disconnecting more as the years go on. Although there are many benefits to using social media, for instance being able to stay connected with friends and family globally, we are lacking real-world engagement. Often, our use of social media can be detrimental to our health, a recent study revealed that those who spent more time online rated higher in depression and anxiety. Interestingly, another study established the number of social media platforms used influenced the participant's mental health. For instance, those who actively use none, one or two social media platforms were less likely to suffer with depression and anxiety when compared to those who actively use 7–11 social media platforms. Researchers have discovered that the more social media platforms used, the more likely the exposure of unfavourable content and the more likely a negative circumstance can unfold. Both contribute to the enhanced deterioration of mental health. Overall, this suggests that not only does the time spent on social media influence our psychological well-being but also the content we are looking at. The reasons for using social media can truly influence our mental health, often we are using social media for the wrong reasons like stalking an ex or comparing ourselves to others. Moreover, we are choosing to neglect and limit our connections and engagements in the real world by either exacerbating our rumination or trying to achieve a short fix of dopamine. It is clearer than ever that social media has a powerful influence over us, it can affect our mental health and our levels of real-world engagement which fundamentally restricts our core human need of connecting. Perhaps by limiting our social media platforms and content exposure, we can lower our mental health issues, step back into the real world and reconnect.

ACTIVITY

If science demonstrates that one way to feel a sense of purpose is through connection, it must be asked, how do we really connect with people? How do we build a secure and meaningful relationship with someone?

To truly be able to gain a sense of meaning and purpose through connection we have learnt that we must communicate, engage and converse. Celeste Headlee, a professional conversationalist, studies meaningful conversation.

As demonstrated through her TED talks, Celeste's research has led her to be able to share tips on having a conversation that encourages connection and therefore enhances the chances of finding a meaning and purpose.

1. Do not multitask.

   Be present with your mind and engaged in the conversation.

2. Enter every conversation assuming that you have something to learn.

   Do not just get your point across as everybody is an expert in something. It is okay to admit you do not know something.

3. Use open-ended questions.

4. Go with the flow.

   Thoughts will come and go but do not focus on thinking of the question to ask.

5. If you do not know, say you do not know.

   Everyone has their own story which is often different to someone else's. Inevitably on our journeys we have learnt different and diverse things. We always have something to learn and a new perspective can always be shared. We may not know what the other person knows and this is okay, in fact it can enhance our connections.

6. Do not equate your experience with theirs, conversations are not a promotional opportunity.

   When someone shares their struggle, we often have a selfish tendency to talk about our similar experiences. This is known as conversational narcissism whereby we turn the focus back on ourselves and our own experiences instead of listening to the speaker and understanding their true feelings. By not equating our problems we can listen and ask questions to help us understand better and connect deeper.

7. Try not to repeat yourself.

8. Stay out of the in-depth detail.

   Dates, times, years and names are a quick bore burner.

9. Listen.

   Do not confuse good talking with good conversing. We must listen in depth but also listen to understand, not to reply.

10. Be brief.
    Short enough to maintain interest but long enough
    to cover a subject.

    It's is on you to shift your attitude, to
    limit your restrictions and increase
    your connections.

    Have you found a meaning to your life?
    Is this you fulfilling your purpose?

Dreams, Desires and Dopamine

Every great dream begins with a dreamer.
Always remember, you have within you the power,
the patience and the passion to reach your dreams.

I have decided to discuss dreams, desires and dopamine (the three Ds) in one chapter as they all have one key commonality, motivation – the drive to success. Needless to say, the more driven you are, the more likely you are to succeed. It is in our innate nature to strive and achieve our personal valued desires. Our motivational drive provides us with an opportunity to change our behaviour, grow interests, develop talents and become more interesting as well as meet interesting people. We can all gain something authentic from being motivated either through personal growth or from valued outcomes. The reason I speak about this is because each of the three Ds holds a unique importance in achieving what you wish to achieve. I will explain this below.

Dreams

Carl Sandburg once said, 'nothing happens unless first we dream'. The journey of anything first starts with a dream. A dream is the primary motivation that creates a vision of our future and enlights a purpose within. Nevertheless, to understand why dreaming plays a significant role in our lives, it is important we recognise how dreaming can help us.

A research paper published by Scarpelli et al., (2019) studied the role of dreams, allowing us to have an insight to the understanding of the inner human world. The researchers highlighted relationships between emotional life experiences and dream experiences. Specifically, dreams have been found to help consolidate our memories and help us to process our emotions. It is possible that dreams construct problem-solving rehearsals that supplement the capability to manage challenging real-life incidents. Neuroimaging studies have also identified that dreaming and emotional salience share a similar neural chemical that controls emotions during wakefulness. In other words, dreams can motivate our waking behaviour and emotions.

In accordance with this scientific research, we realise that just one ability of our inner self has the potency to enrich our life. Whether in wake or sleep, when dreaming consolidates our memories, we are in essence intensifying what we want. When dreaming we process our emotions so that we can gain clarity through assessing how a situation is affecting us. Our emotions are indicators of how safe, secure and stable we feel. Therefore, when dreaming allows us to problem-solve we can make the necessary shifts to ensure that we are aligned contently. When dreaming motivates our wake behaviours and emotions we can determine whether we are making the necessary steps to succeed. If a dream positively motivates our behaviour and emotions, then the likelihood of succeeding is heightened.

Just by dreaming we are already in line with Napoleon Hill when he once said, 'Man, alone, has the power to transform his thoughts into physical reality; man, alone, can dream and make his dreams come true'. It should be noted that one must never give up on a dream just because of the time it will take to accomplish it as the time will pass regardless.

Desires

Desiring something is a vital part to manifesting your dreams. Like dreams, desires change our behaviours and beliefs and both together can bring us positive life experiences. Yet, the crucial element to use our desires to our advantage is to become totally, wholeheartedly obsessed with the dream. When Steven Spielberg was asked about his success he replied, 'I don't dream at night, I dream all day, I dream for a living'. The desire to achieve the dream needs to be so prominent that our cognition becomes so familiar with the vision that even when sleeping we dream about it. The obsession should become so powerful that we eventually reprogramme our brain so that the dream is not just on our mind, it is programmed into our neurological mechanics.

We can all agree that our brains are extraordinarily complex, in fact, scientists have discovered that brain activity is predicted seven seconds ahead of time. It can be argued that before we move a muscle or make a decision, our brain already knows seven seconds before it happens. Interestingly, scientists have also identified unique brain cells that allow us to manufacture decision processes in which we construct our brain's instructions. Evolutionary psychologists have analysed our brains for centuries and have learnt that we have three components that help to explain our conscious brain activity. I will explain how this is relevant to desires and manifesting our dreams.

Part of our brain, known as the neocortex, controls 10% of our mind and is where voluntary thoughts occur. As this is the part of our brain that contains our thoughts and perceptions, we could argue this is our analytical element.

The dominant part of our brain, making up 80%, is the limbic system where involuntary behaviour occurs (essentially the same as a reflex) based on our emotional mindset. Without this part of our brain our neocortex will be overloaded with unnecessary thoughts. The limbic system has the power to influence the Neocortex to repress a particular memory so that we cannot consciously think about it.

The remaining 10% is known as the reptilian brain and runs off our instincts. Here, thoughts are buried so deep that they are completely inaccessible.

The diagram below explains this theory.

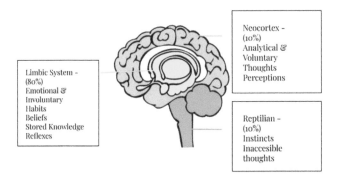

Limbic System –
(80%)
Emotional &
Involuntary
Habits
Beliefs
Stored Knowledge
Reflexes

Neocortex –
(10%)
Analytical &
Voluntary
Thoughts
Perceptions

Reptilian –
(10%)
Instincts
Inaccesible
thoughts

We can think of our mind as an analogy with Google. For instance, our neocortex brain (10%) is the tabs or a site that we are looking at. Whereas our limbic system (90%) is the operating system behind Google; it is the process of bringing forward the relevant sites in accordance with the search. This is illustrated in the diagram below.

Our limbic system is the part of our mind that can recall memories, beliefs, skills, previous experiences. Essentially our limbic system is our data bank, it is the part of our mind that when a sentimental song is played on the radio we can remember exactly where we were and what emotions we were experiencing. Undoubtedly, the limbic system is a powerful part of us that creates 95% of our brain's power. Our limbic system controls our regular body functions such as breathing and our behaviour, without us having any awareness or conscious thought. We can look at our limbic system as an involuntary habit. For example, when someone puts their arms out offering a hug, we tend to mimic the gesture without being consciously aware. Another example of when our limbic system takes over is when we are driving and we get to our destination without remembering how we got there.

The data that is stored in our limbic system is based on two elements, habits and beliefs. Our limbic system will inherently produce behaviour based on our habits and beliefs. What is meant by this is, how we show up is based on what we have learnt or experienced. Let us look at our limbic system beliefs. When we do not believe we have what it takes to achieve our dreams, our limbic system will not seek out the necessary actions. Thus, proving that the belief of the desire is important. If we believe that we can achieve the dream we are a step closer to achieving it. Secondly, our habits are controlled by our limbic system meaning, if we are in a repetitive routine that has little to no benefit towards our dreams, we are not going to achieve them. If we have not yet learnt or experienced a particular factor that helps us achieve our dream, then we must break our habits in order to learn and experience the necessary components that help us achieve our dreams. Despite how much we visualise a dream, without breaking our impractical habits we will not be able to create the actions to achieve. Furthermore, once we believe we can achieve we can begin reassessing our habits and embark the path to achieving our dreams.

We cannot believe that we have transformed our dream into reality until we understand our own magic of imagination and consciousness. You have the power to master your inner mind to achieve your dreams but only if your desire is significantly powerful. Our limbic system is aligned with our emotions while making up our decisions. Therefore, to think of our dreams we must be positively vibrating.

Evidently, our dream starts to become real and manifests when our desire is so strong and consistent that we reprogramme our brain without being consciously aware that we are automatically following directions which concludes to our reality. The desire to achieve a dream has to be incredibly repetitive to reprogramme the thoughts into actions, which in turn will transform the actions into reality.

Dopamine

Dopamine is an organic chemical that we naturally create and that allows us to experience enjoyment and pleasure. When our brain has produced enough dopamine, we experience a natural high and this motivates us to seek out certain behaviours. I speak about dopamine because researchers have identified that dopamine encourages us to desire. It increases our goal-seeking behaviours and curiosities, so we become more motivated to achieve our dreams. With only a small amount of belief that the dream will come true, our dopamine is increased and we become more obsessed with our actions to reach our dream. Given that dopamine can encourage motivated behaviour, dreaming has also been associated with dopamine. When we sleep our brain is disconnected from the external world, despite this, dopamine is still travelling around our brain producing our dream content through our memories and our motivated interests. Some psychologists believe that dreaming is part of our wish fulfilment process with dopamine fuelling the hallucinatory dream content. The famous psychologist Freud once stated, 'it is self-evident that dreams must be a wish-fulfilment since nothing but a wish can set our mental apparatus at work'. To rephrase this, a dream is necessary for dream activity as it provides us with a motivational force. Therefore, the stronger our desire to achieve a dream, the more dopamine is released, the more we are vibrating positive energy into our beliefs and habits, the more likely we are to dream about it as it becomes part of our limbic system; the more likely we are to achieve our dream.

Neuroscientists believe dopamine also provides our ability for something known as motivational salience. Motivational salience is a cognitive process that determines our attention span and it is this that further determines our behaviour. The intensity of our behaviours that encourage us to achieve a dream is regulated by our motivational salience. In particular, the amount of time, energy and risks we allow ourselves to dispense while working for our dream is all determined by our own organic chemical dopamine. Psychologists have also established that dopamine amplifies reward-related memories. Meaning that dopamine strengthens the synapses in our learning and memory part of our brain where neurons can pass on messages. This creates the emotional associations we can experience when we receive a reward. Furthermore, when we experience a positive emotion when achieving a dream, the more likely we are motivated to continue this pleasure-seeking behaviour; in turn making us more driven to achieve our dream. In other words, the more we achieve or even dream to achieve, the more dopamine is released and the more we can feel good and experience pleasurable life experiences.

A study conducted by Dahan et al., (2007), studied rats while sleeping. It was discovered that dopamine activity increased dramatically while the rats were sleeping. The neurophysiological evidence identified that dopamine along with motivational interest was activated during sleep in mammals. Essentially, our dreams are connected to our desires. It could be suggested that our dreams are motivated by our desires and that important motivational goals may possibly be revealed during sleep. Such desired thoughts are related to predictions and expectation which is also related to our dopamine system. Furthermore, a simple dream can change our whole being and in turn, our whole life. We first must start with a dream; this dream enables us to desire, and our desire motivates our dopamine system which converts our energy, so we are highly vibrating.

With all three Ds, we change our behaviours and we become more positive and motivated to achieve our dreams. We must understand that our actions may not always bring happiness but there is no happiness without action.

ACTIVITY

To reinforce each of the three Ds we must take steps to motivate us.

A vision board is a collage of pictures of what we wish to achieve. It allows us to visually see what our life could look like and helps our life to become what we wish it to be. You can cut pictures from magazines or find them on Pinterest and arrange them onto a piece of paper as big or small as you like.

I recently discovered a handy website which has all the tools to make a digital vision board. It is super easy and not as messy as making a vision board out of magazines. Head over to - https://landing.space/

The most important step once you have completed your vision board is to stick it onto the ceiling above your bed so that when you wake up you can start the day envisioning your dream and do the same when you go to bed.

The three Ds allow us to really get to know ourselves so we can identify our dreams and desires and then be able to live the life that is true to us.

If you are unsure about your dreams and desires, then it would be a good idea to pay attention to what you don't want your life to look like and then imagine the exact opposite.

Are you making the necessary actions that transform a dream into reality? Is this you motivating yourself?

Success

Philosophy
[fɪˈlɒsəfi] *noun*
The love of wisdom

What does success mean to you? How do you define success?

Each person's answer will be different to the next person's because success is subjective. For most of us, when we think of success, we think of happiness. We think the vision of our success will automatically make us happy. But what if I were to tell you that your idea of success is a myth?

An ancient Greek philosopher known as Epicurus, taught that happiness is the soul to life. The number one teaching he believed was to do what makes you happy but that you must do so in moderation to avoid suffering from overindulging in what makes your pleasure. Any one person will not become successful if the soul focus is on one aspect of life. You see, it all comes down to balance. If we put all our energy into one desire/interest/dream, then we will face suffering and terrible unhappiness in other aspects of our lives. The lawyer I spoke of in a previous chapter learnt this the hard way; his business was thriving but his family life and health were suffering. There was no balance and the lawyer found himself unhappy despite achieving his dream of running a successful business. We can dream and have a desire to reach our goals but if we do not have balance in doing so, we will destroy everything, not just our own life but the people around who care about us. It must be clear to us that no matter how much we achieve, how many dreams transform to our reality, this will only account for a small percentage of our happiness.

Everything in life comes down to one simple thing which is responsible for all creations – balance. Without the balance of particles, chemicals, gasses and other such elements the Big Bang would not have occurred. Our whole cosmos is formed on balance. Balance is what has made our whole universe. Undoubtedly the universe is our most part of each of our lives because we must observe its natural ways to learn our greatest lessons. Only when we observe nature can we understand balance. The universe is not just the sky, it is the nature that is all around us. For every good we have bad, for every positive we have negative, there is both female and male, rich and poor, created and destroyed. We know that opposites attract and with this we know that it is because of the law of the universe, balance. Even down to the first seeds of life, our world could not have grown; with fire we need water and with water we need air. The universe is created by balance and if we follow the same law, we will find happiness and success. In Greek philosophy it is believed that war is the father of everything. If we view war as conflict and conflict as our balance, we can understand that balance brings our world as one. It is said that nature serves as the foundations of our cosmos. If you exceed the limit of the cosmos, or in other words exceed your own limits; you will experience the most beautiful, but at the same time most disastrous, turn of events. For example, imagine you have built a successful business selling fish globally. You have a high annual turnover and have helped to employ a high number of people. However, over time ecosystems are destroyed and there is a huge detrimental and irreversible environmental impact.

Balance explains everything, including everything around you. If one disregards the universe's limits and dominantly uses the heart in all actions, then we are going against balance and ignoring our ordered cosmos. We will become unbalanced and not gain our happiness or success. Rather we must find our balance, whether that is juggling family life with work or juggling one commitment with another, if we accomplish this balance, we will be happy and successful.

Furthermore, success should be defined as balance.

ACTIVITY

To find our balance we must make a list of what is important to us.

Are there areas of your life that need more attention? Once we have identified the most important things or values of our life then we must act accordingly.

If we look at life in sections it is easier to find and maintain balance. For example, if we section our life into 4 sections,

1. Physical
2. Mental
3. Emotional
4. Spiritual

We can make the effort to fulfil each section but also prioritise each section equally throughout the day and this helps to create balance.

We must make a conscious effort to prioritise this balance and naturally your life will flourish.

Is your life balanced? Is this you working
on your physical, mental, emotional and spiritual self?

Relationships

Love is the greatest force of them all,
it has the power to alter and define our lives.

At the end of the day, we are all emotional beings. We subconsciously abide by the nature of evolution and all crave the same needs in life. No matter our backgrounds, our biology or our aesthetics, we all share one of the innate natural instincts in life – finding a mate. Evolutionally, we search for a mate for the purpose of reproducing and caring for our offspring. Finding a mate was once necessary for survival, the saying 'survive and thrive' was a crucial part of our evolution. Our intense desire to find love stems from our evolution going back through millennials. Finding a mate in life has been hardwired in us through evolution and is now part of our most basic biological and fundamental needs in life. Even though times have changed, we are still a product of evolution despite our personal and modern motives of seeking a mate.

Given our evolutionary and biological mechanisms, we now view finding a mate to be significantly important. There is still a powerful desire to be loved even though perhaps our reasons for finding a mate has changed; we may not want to reproduce; we may just want a strong connection with someone. We naturally crave a connection whether it is an intimate mate or just to feel compatible with someone. It is not surprising that a substantial part of all of us believes that our happiness is reliant on finding a mate and to feel loved and cared for. Surveys have shown that people view having a relationship as one of the top priorities and goals in life. The reason for this was to be able to live a happy and fulfilling life. It is evident that we believe to be happy we must have some form of connection to be able to live a fulfilled life.

In a previous chapter I spoke about connection, now we can start to understand the origins of why connection is so valued. But if the desire for connection is so strong, why do we have the capability to fall in love with one person and not another? According to Dr Kerulis, the attraction of a mate often roots from our patterns of experiences in life which are formed by early childhood experiences. We subconsciously relate our childhood memories and the people within them to who we are meeting in the present. It could be suggested that our compatibility with a mate magnifies through relatedness. Although I believe everything is energy, to find a suitable mate, relatable experiences must have occurred to form a vibration of the same energetic field. The energy we have is magnetic for like energetic people, we have all heard of 'your vibe attracts your vibe'. Therefore, to fall in love or to experience connection we must meet at corresponding energy vibrations in life. If we are all part of the universe made from stars, we must look at the universe for perspective. In cosmology, it is a fact that humans are born ultimately of the stars, for stars to become a cluster they must be symmetrical in characteristics. For stars to cluster they should contain seemingly almost identical metal abundance and contents. Regardless of their aesthetical appearances they can still cluster if they share the same anatomical properties. Us beings work in the same way; we must contain the same anatomical and energetic properties for us to resonate and to form a connection.

Considering our evolution, we know that a major part of our lives is based on connection. I personally view any relationship, whether a friendship or intimate partner, in the form of pillars where we can imagine ourselves as a temple with five pillars holding us up. The diagram below will help you visualise this ideology. I must note, the five pillars that hold me up are stated, however, they may be different to each of your pillars as we all value different things in relationships. Nevertheless, here is the diagram -

For us to have any form of connection with someone there are five pillars that hold us up and allow us to have a healthy connection with another. I know that if all these values are received my pillars are strong and hold me up significantly so that I can have a connection that will flourish and I can gain a sense of fulfilment. However, I also know that if one of these values is missing or perhaps a couple are missing then our pillars start to crumble. I can still have a connection but it will not be as full of abundance. However, the pillars are still holding me up as they have only crumbled. There is still the possibility for the pillars to be fixed and even though there still may remain some evidence of crumbling, we can fix the cracks to stop the pillar from entirely crumbling down. In other words, our connection with another may be hindered but there is still a possibility to work things out. If we decide to work out a crumbling value then we can cement over the cracks, forgive and amend to move on and reach a healthier connection. Of course, with the ordered cosmos we know that everything in life is based upon balance, with what is created also being destroyed. Change is inevitable, perhaps over time one of the pillars or two of the pillars completely crumbles. Depending on which of the pillars crumble, we may still be held up by the other pillars. That is, depending on what we value most, we may still be able to be held up for a connection albeit, not as strong. If the pillars become unbalanced and weak, we can no longer be held up and our connection will disappear. Perhaps, our pillars were never there in the first place and we were based on love (energy) although this is not enough for a temple to stand and exist. As we are emotional beings, we tend to easily forget our values for the fantasy of someone else.

So, what happens when our temple crumbles?

We must simply reread the chapter, searching for meaning and purpose to remind us that with suffering we grow. When we find the materials to rebuild our temple, we will build it to be stronger than the previous temple. To rephrase, when we find our strength and capabilities, we can start to build ourselves up again and we will become a better and stronger person than before.

When we view any relationship in this way, we can become aware of expectations and gain a sense of perception. We also can appreciate our own values and the other person's values. It could be that a way to connect is to identify a person's values and respect their values. For both of your temples to stand up and exist there must be pillars underneath.

To identify our values/pillars and those belonging to another person, we must be observing. Observation is the most underrated skill known to humans. When we observe we can magnify our connection. Observation also helps us to make decisions, informs us with expectations and other such information, helps us to perceive information and allows us to develop our behaviour. With every observation we can understand further and form a deeper connection. If we become observers, we can detect our interactions with another and practice other skills that are unique to connecting with each person.

Observation is not often spoken about and most of us are not aware of the finer details, nor know how to develop our observational skills to achieve deeper connections.

How do we become more observant?

- Improve our concentration by cutting out distractions – especially when speaking with someone. Modern life is indeed full of distractions, when having a conversation with someone try putting your phone away.

- Question everything, be so curious not just in conversation but also by their actions. Sometimes when I mention something that another person does, they often do not know why they do it themselves and other times they do and there you have it; you know something about them that maybe someone else doesn't. You see this is how your connection is instantly deepened. One game that I recommend you all to buy is a card game called *In Too Deep* (it can be purchased on Amazon).
- Record and consider the observations you make about someone and even yourself. This may seem a bit stalkerish but it is often appreciated when you mentally take note of the intricate details. Do not forget that naturally we all crave love.
- Lastly, try new things! How else do you know what you like or what someone else may like. We are built to explore, Carl Sagan says 'humans are evolved to wonder, that understanding is joy, that knowledge is prerequisite to survival'.

ACTIVITY

Undoubtedly we beings need some attributes to become attracted to and to attract. Controversially I am going to say that only a small percentage of what we look like has a role in finding a connection. I believe that there are other important traits, which are supported by science, that help one to be perceived as attractive. I will list these traits below so that we can all use these traits in our daily lives to become more attractive in any form of relationship.

Personality traits and actions to make you become more attractive:

1. Being present – live in the moment
2. Vulnerability
3. Genuineness
4. Good sense of humour
5. Creativeness
6. Natural curiosity
7. Optimism
8. Good communicator
9. Knowledgeable
10. Casual touches
11. Be available
12. Open mindedness
13. Assertiveness
14. Maintain good eye contact

15. Smile often
16. Have deep meaningful discussions – A card game called 'In Too Deep' can help with meaningful conversations.
17. Mirror them
18. Always learn new things and share them
19. Be kind
20. Be generous
21. Be humble
22. Be self-aware
23. Tilt your head to the side when someone is being vulnerable
24. Check up on them and their friends when in the right position to
25. Be a little mysterious
26. Use their name often
27. Listen and repeat their phrases
28. Observe and remember the little details
29. Eat healthy
30. Polite with good manners.

Have you identified your values?
Is this you being valued and valuing others?

Generosity and Gratitude

I do not need therapy, I need love.

Generosity

As a matter of course, love is a desire that most of us crave. What if we play devil's advocate and look at the effect of loving? Along with seeking someone to love, we also seek someone to love and care for. It is regarded to be true that our desire to love is equally strong as seeking to be loved. We naturally tend to love and care, this tendency is illuminated when we see a dog or a baby. Some of us adopt a pet to fulfil our own need of seeking something to love and care for. As much as our evolution plays a role in inheriting our desire to be loved, it could be considered that we share the same inherent biology to love. Researchers have proposed the basis of living and caring derives from a fulfilment of happiness. Both expressing love and being generous are associated with our happiness levels. The giver and the receiver both benefit from love and generosity.

Intriguingly, a study reveals that just from a small act of kindness generates equal amounts of happiness when compared to significant acts. Some of the study participants were granted £5 and the others £20. Both groups were asked to spend the money on themselves or on someone else. The participants who spent the money on someone else experienced higher levels of happiness than those who spent the money on themselves. What is more, the amount of money spent on others did not interfere with the amount of happiness the participant experienced. Evidently, the power of loving is important for our happiness. To increase our own levels of happiness we must be more generous in all aspects of life, including our time, it does not have to include any expenditure and can cost you nothing. We need to give more and spend time connecting, little gifts of generosity go further than you can imagine. It was Mother Teresa who said, 'it is more important to do small things with great love than to do great things with little love'.

<u>Gratitude</u>

It is now well known that gratitude can enhance our happiness. People are now practising gratitude more than ever before. Gratitude is often said to be the core practice to a happy and fulfilling life. If we practice gratitude correctly, we can distinguish our perspective and become more mindful of this.

Ultimately, we can narrow our perspectives down to two universal views:

1. We have all been granted with the blessing to experience life, to create how we wish, to think freely, to love. If the things in my life were taken away or if I were to wake up living someone else's life, then I will miss how I experienced life.

2. I deserve more, I will never settle. There is always someone else out there who has a better car or more money and I can be like them too. Material things motivate me. I have what I have but I would like more.

One of these perspectives empowers us for a more meaningful life. The other perspective authorises us for momentary happiness. A happiness that is materialised artificially.

If you guessed correctly, the better perspective to practice is the first perspective. We must be appreciative of what we have rather than living in the future and what the future could bring. When we live in the future and think that our future is what is going to bring us happiness, we are only chasing an illusion. Our mind makes synthetic happiness with endless success. This way of thinking is what sets us up for unhappiness. We think that if we get a certain car, we will receive infinite amounts of happiness. Rather, we buy the car and our happiness levels increase for a period but decrease faster than when we find happiness in nature. Then of course, there is the next craving for something else which spirals into an inexhaustible search for happiness that is never entirely achieved.

True happiness can only be found and felt when we slow life down. Slowing life down allows us to appreciate the smaller things in life that bring us the greatest amount of organic happiness. If we live fast-paced lives, naturally we do not notice the things we are blessed with as our mind is always thinking of the next matter. The future has not yet happened and as much as we try to predict it, we never know what is coming. Therefore, we must appreciate what we have, slow it down and show our gratitude for what life is and what it blesses with us every day. When we slow life down, we can enjoy the benefits we receive to live a happier and fulfilling life.

Albeit, more so than ever, we have adapted to expecting the unexpected with our worlds having been exposed to vast amounts of unfortunate events. Such events have caused us enormous grief, anxiety and stress. Despite life naturally continuing after each tragedy, we are left picking up the pieces that we have helplessly encountered. The national COVID pandemic forced us to find and adjust to new ways of living which has not been easy for some of us. During this two-year long national pandemic we have had riots, protests, poverty, a rise in mental health issues, greater amounts of domestic abuse cases that have been exposed, the NHS and social services working way past their breaking point and more! Regardless of the era we are experiencing, there are always vast amounts of chaos. Undoubtedly, life has not been easy. Yet only now are we facing the consequences with a huge backlog and worryingly high inflation. The repercussions are immense, it is so easy to drown in the negativity of adversity.

With this in mind, on a daily basis, social media increasingly allows us to consume high expectations of ourselves through watching other people, people that we may not even know. We have become brainwashed into believing that happiness only lies in achieving self-enhancing goals whether it is career success, fame, wealth or power. Despite natural and external events, we also face pressure in consistently bettering ourselves and our lives to feel worthy, to feel respected and to feel enough.

Yet the need to love and care for others is rarely emphasised and reiterated. Our innate core human need to love and care is barely even acknowledged and spoken about. While we endure excessive challenges and suffering, we must look within to know how we can bring ourselves to see the light at the end of the tunnel. Slowing life down and attending to our core human needs of loving and caring we can start to recognise the blessings in our life and express our gratitude. Epicurus proclaimed we should not spoil what we have by desiring what we have not; remember that what you now have and who you are was once among the things you only hoped for.

ACTIVITY

As cliche as it sounds, I am going to tell you to start a gratitude list.

At the beginning of every day write three things for which you are grateful.

At the end of every day write one highlight of your day.

If you get stuck with expressing your gratitude, you can do this in reverse and ask yourself if you didn't have a certain thing in your life then what would your life look like?

Secondly, we should oblige ourselves to execute acts of kindness.

To enhance our generosity and fulfil our basic human needs, one can take up their duty to give. Here is a brief list of acts of kindness that may inspire your activity:

1. Donate your time for an afternoon teaching something you enjoy
2. Pay for someone's parking
3. Plant a tree
4. Do a beach clear up
5. Help someone with their bags
6. Let someone go in front of you in a queue

7. Buy someone flowers
8. Listen to someone
9. Compliment someone
10. Put a love letter of encouragement on someone's car
11. Buy someone an ice cream
12. Buy something small but thoughtful for someone
13. Spend time with your family
14. Send care packages
15. Donate
16. Leave a note in your loved one's lunch box
17. Lend a book
18. Send colouring books to kids in hospital
19. Help where you can
20. Make someone something.

How have you slowed your life down?
Is this you loving life?

Dark Energy

If dark matter and dark energy are 95% of
everything, shouldn't we be asking more about it?
Shouldn't we be learning as much as we can about it?

Everything ever observed by astronomers and physicists has been solely normal matter. Normal matter is the visible universe, it includes the earth, the sun, galaxies and the stars. We know that all of these are made up of protons, neutrons and electrons which are bunched together making what is known as atoms. To today's date, all discoveries totals to only 5% of the universe. Everything that we can observe from trees to whales to the skies above is only 5% of the entire universe. The remaining 95% remains mysterious. Interestingly, despite this dark mystery being invisible, physicists have discovered that our universe is made up of 27% dark matter and 68% dark energy.

We know that 13.8 billion years ago the Big Bang happened. During the first few minutes of the Big Bang hydrogen and helium were created. Yet underlying this was dark matter. Dark matter existed before the formation of the stars. As the density of the Big Bang grew, hydrogen and helium fragmented out. From this cooling of gasses, stars were formed which gave light to the universe. Billions of years after the origin of the universe, dark matter pulled in more mass. Dark matter multiplied accompanied by more stars and gas, in turn formed more rings of dark matter. As the years went on, astronomers realised that dark matter had to have significantly powerful properties as it was clear that dark matter dominated the gravitational pulls of the cosmos. Dark matter was simply deciding which galaxies could evolve. Indeed, without dark matter it would have been next to impossible for stars and galaxies to begin to form. Dark matter has shaped our entire universe.

Alongside dark matter, dark energy is everywhere, really. It is between the galaxies. It is in the room you are in, wherever you are it surrounds you every millisecond of each day. It is believed that everywhere that there is empty space, dark energy is there. Therefore, empty space is not truly empty as dark energy travels and fluctuates in and out of our existence on tiny, minute scales.

So, what is the difference between dark energy and dark matter?

While they may be related, it appears that their effects are different.

Dark matter accounts for one quarter of the universe and pulls matter inwards. It also exerts its influence on individual galaxies.

Dark energy accounts for 68% of the total mass and energy of the universe. It is by far the dominant mysterious force. Dark energy pushes matter outward, it is the opposite of gravity. Dark energy exerts its influence on the largest cosmic scale.

For the most part, our universe is made up of dark energy, for our cosmic universe to evolve, dark energy must have been a significant element. Because of dark energy our universe is continually expanding, perhaps this motion is creating further magic.

The importance of dark energy in our day-to-day life remains a mystery however, if dark energy is so crucial in the creation of the universe, surely, its power may have some sort of influence on us. If the nature of dark energy is not explained, then our open-mindedness is expanded to depths of how dark energy contributes to our lives. For the entirety of our universe, is it not great that dark energy is just one mysterious force that has helped create us and our world? What else is dark energy and dark matter creating? What else is possible? The thoughts are endless. A mysterious cosmic element that appears to support our existence and helps us survive on a daily basis; what other magic does the universe surround us with? There were once no galaxies, stars, planets, or civilisations in our universe. Our world was once non-existent and then inhabited, now our world is overflowing with life. With the power of dark matter and dark energy, over billions of years we have transformed and we are only a microscopic segment; and we have only revealed a glimpse of our entire cosmos. We must trust the abundant powers of the universe as it has blessed us immensely already.

ACTIVITY

In times of trouble, we must remain faithful in trusting we are right where we need to be. The universe has guided us to where we are right at this very moment, surely that confirms our peace.

Often before manifesting or experiencing any kind of growth we may feel doubtful, insecure and unsettled. Just like when we physically grow, we must experience some sort of growing pains but we wait it out and in time we grow taller. When we experience pain, we expect to grow and after a while we grow. We should be as consistently patient with our fate. When we are in doubt, facing frustration and feel lost, we must ask the universe to show us a sign that we are still connected and being guided to our destiny. Pick a song or a sign or animal and in the duration of your struggles, ask the universe to show you your sign if you are on the right path. You will be surprised by the responsiveness of the universe and the speed the universe will reveal its reassurance.

Mantra: 'I am right where I need to be, I continue to put all my trust in the universe to guide me on my journey in life.'

Is this you trusting the universe?

The Great Universal Conscious

As a part, you inhere in the Whole. You will vanish
into that which gave you birth; or rather,
you will be transmuted once more into the creative
reason of the universe.

As we know, we are made up of atoms that originate from
the Big Bang. Earlier I mentioned of dark matter showering
us with its magic, I did not mention that matter is also
within us. To our advantage, when the universe was
created, matter also condensed itself into our creation.
Matter transforms into life when the required conditions
occur. Just like our human conditions for creating a baby,
an egg must be fertilised by a sperm, for matter to create
life it must be met with other such atoms. Interestingly,
recent research has discovered that matter holds memory.
During our journey of life, we learn and we make
memories. Theorists believe that the matter within us will
eventually vanish into the universe when we die and this
matter due to its memory will be recycled into another
being. If I rephrase this in simple terms, we hold memories,
and these memories are transferred during our death and in

turn they cluster with other atoms until eventually a new being is born with the same atoms that created us. This cycle continues infinitely. All the knowledge of an atom is transferred and this process is the explanation for why the unexplainable may occur. Think of it as a stream, all our deceased atoms find themselves in a stream that flows in an orderly fashion until eventually the atoms build up and at the end of the stream a new being is rebirthed. For nothing comes from nothing or can return to nothing.

On the occasion of death, one's particles do not drop out of the universe, they remain in the universe. After death, atoms undergo a process of change to resolve into several particles. The atoms are reformed with the same elements which formed the universe and us. You see now that we are all one, we all share the same atoms that formed our universe as we are part of the universe. To become who we are we have undergone change, yet change is not often appreciated. Regardless, if change is perceived to be uncomfortable and anxiety fuelled, without change occurring nothing can come to life. Even to the most minute details in life, could we have had a hot bath if the water did not undergo change? Could we be nourished if the food did not experience change? We must appreciate the cycles of our orderly universe, as is it really possible for any useful thing to be achieved without change? Do you not see, then, that change yourself is of the same order and no less necessary to nature?

As atoms are indestructible, we must consist of formal atoms. Consequently, every part of each of us will one day be recycled and transferred into the universe. Which in turn will again change into yet another being and so on for infinity. It is the same process in which each of us were created and how our parents and grandparents were created.

When we face hostility, we must remember that we all came from the same one source, we are all no better than another, we simply are alone in our universe to make our own decisions. Superiority of a being does not occur, there is not one person that is more special than one other, whether they have more fame, wealth or power. We all exist through recycled atoms. Yet the one thing that defines us is the decisions we make and the amount of goodness we choose to exert. One must not judge others for the reality they choose to create. We must stay humble as, all is one, all of us are part of the one universe due to our transferable atoms. We all originate from the same universe, we all share the same atoms, we all have been the product of recycled atoms and we all follow the natural equilibrium of the orderly universe. No matter your belief in the creation of civilisation on earth, all beliefs originate from the one same source. Everything is one, one great universal consciousness is the creator of all.

ACTIVITY

Think of the countless changes in which you have experienced, relate it to how the universe changes.

List down the changes you have experienced over your lifetime and write next to each change the feelings you felt and perhaps still feel when experiencing this change.

Now you must realise that life is only an opinion, there is nothing either good or bad it is your mind that creates the associated emotion. This power of thought is universal, we all share the same thought patterns which in turn highlights that we are all one, all fellow citizens. We all are mutually associated with the one great universal consciousness.

Are you radiating good vibes?
Is this you creating your reality?

You

It is not of value what stone walls, houses, cars or riches the man leaves behind, it is important what one left by his heart for those who were left behind. How people remember you, the good you served, how you influenced and inspired people is defined as your riches.

You have now reached the last chapter of this book so by now, beyond any doubt, it should be realised the power YOU hold. You have magical particles inside of you, dark matter that is so powerful it created the universe. Not only are you created by powerful atoms but you are also constantly surrounded by the magic of dark matter. You are part of the universe, the same one universe that is omnipotent.

You are created through recycled atoms, you share the same elements as Elon Musk, Einstein, Oprah, Richard Branson. You are a powerful being, you have the same particles within you and therefore the same potential to be as powerful as the most powerful people.

Just because something is difficult for you, do not therefore suppose it to be beyond mortal power. On the contrary, if anything is possible and proper for man to do, assume that it must fall within your own capacity.

You are the energy that sustains the universe. You have a purpose in this universe, a purpose that is unique to you. Does the Sun think to do the rain's work? No one can fulfil your purpose even if they are like you, or perhaps you view them as better. What about the stars? They are all different but do the same work and yet they all come out together to shine.

You are not made worse or better by praise. Do diamonds shine brighter with praise? Does a rose lose its beauty for lack of admiration?

You are what holds the almighty power that decides how you glow, how you live, how you behave and how you create your reality. No one else can make these choices.

Is this you believing?

Is This You?

Katy Knapman is the author of Is This You.

She earned her Bachelor of Science in Psychology and is also the author of a pharmacological article. She has contributed her research to implement scientific knowledge and continues to do so. When she is not researching and writing in the tranquillity of the Kent countryside, Katy spends most of her time somewhere in the world with a paintbrush in hand and a set of watercolours.

Keep in touch and up-to-date with Katy via Instagram - @katy_knapman_

Lightning Source UK Ltd.
Milton Keynes UK
UKHW020742261122
412824UK00012B/281

9 781803 811741